IMAGES
of America

FORT SILL

Welcome home! The Hannifan family—from left to right, Tim Sr., Tim Jr., Zoe, Kelley, and Seth—pose for their picture on January 17, 2014, as recently promoted Staff Sergeant Hannifan makes a surprise appearance to his children's Flower Mound Elementary School in Lawton upon his return from an overseas deployment to the United Arab Emirates. He was a member of the 2nd Battalion, 5th Field Artillery Regiment at Fort Sill. (Courtesy of Tim Hannifan Sr.)

On the Cover: Independence Day and other holidays were celebrated boisterously on the frontier. In this c. 1890 tug-of-war, participants lie on the sidewalk as rival teams exert themselves for success. Participants—soldier, civilian, and Indian alike—often placed their bets so high that to lose meant impoverishment. (Courtesy of Fort Sill National Historic Landmark.)

IMAGES
of America

FORT SILL

Mark K. Megehee
Foreword by Dr. Boyd L. Dastrup

ARCADIA
PUBLISHING

ISBN 978-1-4671-2964-0

Published by Arcadia Publishing
Charleston, South Carolina

Printed in the United States of America

Library of Congress Control Number: 2018934262

For all general information, please contact Arcadia Publishing:
Telephone 843-853-2070
Fax 843-853-0044
E-mail sales@arcadiapublishing.com
For customer service and orders:
Toll-Free 1-888-313-2665

Visit us on the Internet at www.arcadiapublishing.com

This book is dedicated to the men and women stationed at the military post of Fort Sill, both in peace and war, from its founding in 1869 to the present day and beyond.

Contents

Foreword		6
Acknowledgments		7
Introduction		8
1.	Early Years	11
2.	A New Mission, A New City	55
3.	Camp Doniphan and Over There	67
4.	Cradle of Army Aviation	79
5.	The Challenge of World War II and Korea	83
6.	The Cold War Years	91
7.	The Mission Enhanced	101
8.	The Past Lives On	111

Foreword

Although Fort Sill is noted for being the premier artillery training ground for both air defense artillery and field artillery, its origins extend into the 19th century. From the first contact with the US Army in the 1830s, when Col. Henry Dodge led an expedition to meet with the Comanches near present-day Fort Sill through the rest of the 1800s, the post served primarily as a cavalry post. During the Red River Indian Wars on the southern Great Plains in the 1870s, cavalry columns chased down bands of Comanches and eventually forced them to move onto the reservation surrounding Fort Sill. Once this was done, Fort Sill moved into a new era. From the post, cavalry soldiers patrolled western Indian Territory to maintain the peace and to prevent white intrusion.

The great cavalry tradition ended early in the 20th century, when the 29th Artillery Battery arrived at Fort Sill. This marked the beginning of the post's transition to a noted field artillery training post. In 1911, the War Department opened the School of Fire for Field Artillery. From World War I through the second decade of the 21st century, the post was synonymous with field artillery training; was a leader in the development of field artillery tactics, doctrine, and organization; and was a key player in the development of field artillery weapons and equipment.

Congress passed the Base Relocation and Consolidation Act in 2005, leading Fort Sill to add an air defense artillery mission in 2009. This caused the US Army Training and Doctrine Command to designate Fort Sill as the Fires Center of Excellence. Now, the post provides air defense and field artillery training and serves as the US Army's focal point in the development of fires capabilities and targeting.

Weaving together an insightful narrative with outstanding images, Mark Megehee tells the story of the post's colorful past. Carefully selected images from various historical photographic collections take readers on a journey into the past and bring them into the present. Such a pictorial history gives readers a vivid glimpse into Fort Sill's history.

—Dr. Boyd L. Dastrup
Command Historian
US Army Field Artillery School

Acknowledgments

Fort Sill is not only a crucial military asset but also a most amazing combination of the old and the new. Regarding the latter, I am indebted to my photographer, Peter J. Contos, who combined his expertise in photography with his appreciation for the historic sites of Fort Sill. I wish to thank the following institutions and their staffs for making available the photographs and other illustrations that made this publication possible: Frank J. Siltman, director and chief executive officer of the Museums of Fort Sill; curator Dr. Scott Neel and museum specialists Erik Radowski and Robert L. Anderson Jr. of the Fort Sill National Historic Landmark and Museum for their generous and in-depth cooperation in providing the lion's share of photographs and supporting illustrations for this work; historian Dr. Boyd Dastrup and librarian Shelia Duckworth of the Fort Sill Command Historian's Office and Morris Swett Library for reviewing the narrative and offering historical insight; curator Gordon Blaker and exhibits specialist Zane Mohler of the Fort Sill US Army Artillery Museum for extensive access to archival photographs and verification of details; Rod Roadruck for assistance with historic photographs; *Fort Sill Tribune* editor James A. Brabenec; public affairs officer Joel McFarland of the Reynolds Army Health Clinic; and John D. Beemer of the Fires Center of Excellence Office of Protocol.

I am also indebted to Col. Gene Love of the Armed Services YMCA in Lawton, Oklahoma, for suggestions and general guidance involving the recent history of Fort Sill. Finally, I am most grateful to my wife, Georgia, who provided timely clerical support and skills.

Unless otherwise noted, all images appear courtesy of the Fort Sill National Historic Landmark and Museum in Fort Sill, Oklahoma.

INTRODUCTION

Native Americans called this land "the place where mountains meet the plains." These mountains came to be called the Wichitas after a tribe of American Indians who were the first to settle in the area. They managed to coexist peacefully with the fierce Comanches, Kiowas, and other warring tribes of the region.

The first military intrusion upon the southern plains occurred in 1834. Col. Henry Dodge and the 1st US Dragoons briefly occupied the future site of Fort Sill, which was dubbed Camp Comanche. Relations between soldiers and tribesmen remained peaceful and led to the first treaty of peace between the United States and the indigenous Native Americans of the Southwest.

In 1852, Army explorers Capt. Randolph Marcy and Lt. George B. McClellan surveyed the Red River region, mapped the countryside, and suggested a permanent fort in the district. The proposal was repeated six years later by Col. Douglas Cooper, whose Chickasaw Indians scouted the area.

Gen. Philip Sheridan concentrated three cavalry regiments and some infantry just east of Medicine Bluffs in late December 1868 in the aftermath of Lt. Col. George A. Custer's attack on an Indian village, known as the Battle of the Washita. Other nearby sites were considered for a fort, but this was selected for its defensible terrain, good supply of water and timber, and strategic location.

The new post was staked out, and rudimentary construction commenced in January 1869. It was initially styled Camp Comanche, although some 10th Cavalry Buffalo Soldiers called it Camp Starvation, only half-jokingly. In early summer, General Sheridan assigned it the name Fort Sill after Brig. Gen. Joshua Sill, a fellow West Point classmate killed during the Civil War.

The first post commander, Col. Benjamin Grierson, supervised construction. The 10th Cavalry men worked hard, and nondescript shelters gave way to semi-permanent picket houses. These formed the eastern side of the parade ground quadrangle. From 1869 to 1871, most of the barracks, officers' quarters, and related buildings were erected. For these permanent structures, limestone was quarried a mile to the southeast, then laboriously hauled uphill.

Hostilities with formidable tribes, including the Comanches, Kiowas, Plains Apaches, Southern Cheyenne, and Arapahos, characterized the early years of the fort. Skirmishes and battles were fought to safeguard communications, trade, and nearby settlers. The Red River War was the last military campaign on the southern Great Plains, from 1874 to 1875. Converging columns of bluecoat soldiers ultimately compelled the recalcitrant tribal leaders to sue for peace. Fort Sill and Camp Supply to the north were crucial components in the campaign. To ensure a lasting peace, Fort Elliott in the Texas Panhandle and Fort Reno were also established.

This war forced the surrender of virtually all those Indian warriors who had struggled for so long to maintain or reclaim their ancestral lands. Defeated, with weapons and ponies surrendered, the tribesmen and their families returned to their indicated reservations. They unwillingly accepted the White Man's Road.

By the 1880s, Fort Sill's garrison dwindled; congressional appropriations diminished as peace was well established. Yet an upsurge of importance arose when the War Department decided to settle the Chiricahua Apaches of Geronimo's band at Fort Sill. After his surrender in Arizona in 1886, Geronimo's warriors and their dependents had been held as prisoners of war, some in Florida and some in Alabama. The climate and other conditions led to serious losses, and in 1894, they were reunited and transported to Fort Sill.

They remained prisoners of war until 1913, four years after the passing of Geronimo. Land was provided them by the Kiowas and Comanches, and they were placed under the care of Lt. Hugh L. Scott. In the years that followed, they prospered. Some gardened, some raised stock, and others joined the US Army. Troop L, 7th Cavalry, became a model of efficiency and an example of the benefits that could be rendered by experienced Indian scouts. In 1897, Geronimo himself enlisted and served as a US scout.

As the 19th century passed into the 20th, change was in the air. One significant transition took place among the American Indian tribes surrounding Fort Sill: missionaries from multiple denominations evangelized the tribes, winning many converts. Gradually, old tribal ways were modified. Rev. Frank H. Wright established a mission in the so-called "Punchbowl," just north of Fort Sill. He labored on behalf of the Dutch Reformed Church, preaching in camp meetings and wherever he could muster some interest. Rev. J.B. Wicks, from the Episcopal Diocese of New York, preached in the area as early as 1881. Roman Catholic Fr. Isidore Robot was active from Fort Sill to Anadarko. The Baptists opened a church at Rainy Mountain. The Methodists opened one at Anadarko and the Mennonites one at Post Oak Creek, to the west of Fort Sill. A number of Native Americans not only embraced Christianity but also inspired their people as ministers of the gospel.

In civil affairs, a major city arose adjacent to Fort Sill in 1901. Lawton resulted from the last of the Kiowa, Comanche, and Apache lands being declared open for settlement. Instead of a land run, a lottery for 160-acre allotments was held. About 6,500 names were drawn from the 29,000 registered. The home of one fortunate, Mattie Beal, has even been preserved. The city of Lawton was formed almost overnight, with an estimated population of 25,000 living in tents.

Only a small garrison of cavalry remained at Fort Sill at the beginning of the 20th century. Someone suggested closing the fort and giving the land to the Fort Sill Apaches. Abandonment seemed imminent.

However, in 1902, the 29th Field Artillery Battery arrived, and before long, the idea took root for Fort Sill to become a training center for artillery. The spacious and varied terrain was ideal for artillery practice and maneuvers.

A provisional regiment of field artillery was organized from various detachments in 1905. The last troops of cavalry departed within the next few years, and the School of Fire for Field Artillery was established in 1911. Its founder and first commandant was Capt. Dan T. Moore.

In 1908, plans were laid to demolish the old limestone buildings and historic structures to make way for modernization. These were saved when Secretary of War William H. Taft inspected the post. After spending the night in Sherman House, with its long association of military commanders, he said "You need worry no longer. We will not change a single stone of the Old Post." Aside from the loss of some subsidiary structures, the Old Post Quadrangle (OPQ) and outlying buildings remain intact.

In the years that followed, New Post facilities arose to the west of the OPQ as Fort Sill took up the mission of the branch of field artillery, the "King of Battle." In addition to field training, officers were developed in the classroom, and new weapons were tested and compared with those of other nations. Chief of field artillery Maj. Gen. William J. Snow organized and coordinated the School of Field Artillery, paving the way for victory in two world wars.

The approach of World War I led to the School of Musketry (1913–1918), where multitudes of soldiers trained as infantry. Sprawling Camp Doniphan covered vast acres to the west and prepared over 50,000 soldiers of several specialties to go "over there."

The post hospital was expanded and modernized; its facilities were state-of-the-art and personnel second to none. The capacity was increased to be able to receive and care for much larger numbers of patients, particularly in the event of war.

Army aviation truly began at Fort Sill. The 1st Aero Squadron, composed of Curtiss Jennies, arrived in 1915. This signaled the beginning of the Army's cross-country missions. Other squadrons followed as artillery observation, aerial mapping, and tactical photography developed.

In 1917, Henry Post Army Airfield was completed, which witnessed a wide range of missions, including training for war and aerial feats. Balloon operations pioneered new techniques as wooden hangars were replaced with a steel structure in 1935. The testing of experimental aircraft was exciting and drew great interest from the American public. Although the Army aviation mission was relocated to Fort Rucker, Alabama, in 1954, Fort Sill retains significant aviation capability.

Throughout the 20th century, Fort Sill has excelled in training soldiers to suppress targets on the modern battlefield. Commanders like Lt. Gen. Lesley J. McNair have provided innovative leadership, whether in organization, training, or technological opportunities. Achievements like the Fire Direction Center and the adoption of ENIAC (the world's first successful computer) placed Fort Sill at the forefront of international excellence in artillery.

The 2005 Base Relocation and Consolidation Act concentrated all artillery fire development, training, and expertise at Fort Sill. The air defense artillery branch departed Fort Bliss, Texas, and completed its transition in 2011. The two branches prospered in a community long known for appreciation of the military. With colocation of the Air Defense Artillery School and the Field Artillery School at Fort Sill, the US Army Training and Doctrine Command designated Fort Sill as the Fires Center of Excellence to become the premier artillery training ground for the free world, involving all fire missions. Throughout the 20th century, it excelled in training soldiers from over 50 countries. It possesses an amazing tradition of resilience and performance, and proudly remembers its past.

One

Early Years

The first 40 years of Fort Sill involved a peace-keeping mission enforced chiefly by cavalrymen assisted by some infantry. The 1867 Medicine Lodge Treaty bound the tribes of the southern plains to well-defined reservations and curtailed both the hunting of game and the raiding of enemies outside of those boundaries. Unfortunately, the tribesmen, particularly those of traditionally warlike tribes, were unable to subsist on their reduced domains and were unwilling to forego the age-old prerogatives of war.

Founded in 1869, Fort Sill sent forth soldiers to quell depredations committed by those warriors who left their reservations and raised havoc. Hostilities involved the Comanche, Kiowa, Southern Cheyenne, and Arapahos, who attacked buffalo hunters, freight men, travelers, and settlers throughout the region.

Gen. Philip Sheridan resolved to establish a permanent installation possessing defensible terrain, adequate timber, and a reliable source of water. He selected the site for the new Army post, which some called Camp Medicine Bluffs and others Camp Wichita; after about six months, it was officially designated Fort Sill.

The gallant African American soldiers of the 10th Cavalry Regiment, known as Buffalo Soldiers, managed to conduct punitive operations against restive tribesmen even while absorbed in the hard labor involved in constructing the new fort.

The extermination of the vast herds of buffalo led to the end of tribal prosperity and reshaped tribal culture. The resulting Red River War ended the last effort to return to former ways among tribal warriors and their dependents. In 1875, the last Indian holdouts were compelled to surrender and return to their reservations.

Fort Sill was selected for an additional responsibility in the 1890s. Geronimo's band of Apaches, held as prisoners of war in either Florida or Alabama since 1886, was placed under its custody. Despite a meager beginning, the Fort Sill Apache prisoners of war flourished; their industrious pursuit of the White Man's Road was an unqualified success.

The closing years of the 19th century witnessed Christian missions among the tribes in the region. Churches resulted, with Native American congregations appearing in all the surrounding tribes, whether formerly warlike or peaceful. White Bible workers continued their labors among these flocks and were assisted or replaced by tribal evangelists, ministers, and pastors.

Beheading Mountain and adjacent Cut Throat Gap were the site of an infamous massacre in 1833. A Kiowa band led by Chief Ah-da-te was surprised in a dawn attack by hundreds of Osage warriors. Most of the Kiowa fighting men were away on an expedition against the Utes. The sacred medicine bundle, or *tai-me*, fell into enemy hands, and one estimate placed the number of Kiowa dead at over 150, many of whom were women and children. Brass cooking kettles were gathered into the center of the camp, and dozens of severed heads were placed in them as an offering to the Osage Great Spirit.

Tribal unrest, such as the Cut Throat Gap Massacre, awakened the US Army's interest in the southern plains. An expedition comprising 400 dragoons under the command of Col. Henry Dodge explored present-day southwest Oklahoma. Relations remained friendly, especially as two ransomed girls were returned to their people, one Wichita and one Kiowa.

Camp Comanche was the site where the US dragoons of Colonel Dodge positioned themselves while preliminary talks were held pursuant to a lasting treaty of peace. Honors were exchanged between the horse soldiers and the fierce "Lords of the Plains," as the Comanches were known. The adjacent Comanche village featured over 200 lodges.

This grass house was typical of the style of shelter favored by the Wichita Indians. The first tribe known to settle in this area, the Wichitas were peaceful and agricultural though seminomadic. The terms of the peace resulting from the dragoon expedition permitted them to continue to reside in the vicinity east of Medicine Bluffs, precisely where Fort Sill would be established 33 years later.

Capt. Randolph Marcy explored the region in 1852 and produced an excellent map. He named several prominent streams and landmarks, including Mount Scott. He and subordinate officers climbed the southern slopes of Medicine Bluffs as well as the knoll upon which Fort Sill would be situated. Captain Marcy recommended the site for a military post.

The Tar Pit, located two miles east of the site of Fort Sill, was examined by Captain Marcy. He related that Native Americans used the tar for curative treatments, applied it to the backs of their ponies, and used it as glue to secure arrowheads to their arrows. In modern times, it has been declared the oldest tar pit in North America, yielding specimens up to 250 million years old.

Lt. Col. George A. Custer commanded the 7th Cavalry Regiment in the aftermath of the Civil War. He was rescued from presidential disfavor and brought west to fight Indians by his patron, Gen. Philip Sheridan. He made a devastating attack upon the unsuspecting Cheyenne village of Peace Chief Black Kettle, near the Washita River, in November 1868.

The aftermath of Custer's attack at the Washita was a successful evasion from superior hostile forces. Fifty-three Cheyenne prisoners were force-marched in wintry weather to Camp Supply, Indian Territory. Meanwhile, Osage scouts reported the loss of Maj. Joel Elliott and his entire command (18 total), who had been surrounded and slain during the recent action.

Osage warriors served as scouts from the time of the dragoon expedition through the Civil War and during Custer's campaign of 1868–1869. Charging Hawk posed for this portrait about 1869. He holds his M1860 cavalry saber, reminiscent of the long knives used at Cut Throat Gap over 30 years previously.

Maj. Gen. Philip H. Sheridan, commander of the Department of Missouri, coordinated the assault on the tribes of the southern plains in 1868–1869. On January 8, 1869, he selected the site for a permanent Army post strategically located in the midst of warlike tribes. The general himself staked out the boundaries, assisted by Pvt. Johnny Murphy, his ambulance driver, for what would become Fort Sill. (Courtesy of Morris Swett Library, Fires Center of Excellence.)

Brig. Gen. Joshua W. Sill was a West Point classmate of Gen. Philip H. Sheridan. He won rapid promotion during the Civil War, earning distinction in the western theater. He lost his life leading a charge at the Battle of Stones River on December 31, 1862. Camp Wichita became Fort Sill by order of General Sheridan.

Col. Benjamin H. Grierson commanded the 10th Cavalry Regiment, one of the regiments of the famed Buffalo Soldiers. He became the first post commander, putting his soldiers, along with civilian carpenters and stone masons, to the arduous task of constructing temporary and then permanent buildings for the new post. The fort was virtually complete when he departed for a new assignment in 1872. (Courtesy of Morris Swett Library, Fires Center of Excellence.)

Medicine Bluffs was sacred to the surrounding tribes, who made medicine from the flora in the vicinity. Some warriors achieved their vision quest there. The terrain was explored by the Buffalo Soldiers from early 1869 onwards. While some soldiers scaled the 300-foot escarpment, others discovered a den of rattlesnakes amid the crevices. Perhaps a hundred snakes were killed, and their rattles were used to adorn the soldiers' hats.

Quinette Crossing of Medicine Bluffs Creek was the site of the original headquarters of Camp Wichita. The small white marker indicates the location of General Sheridan's tent. Colonel Grierson's picket house, which included both his quarters and office, was at the top of the hill in the left background in this c. 1943 view. (Courtesy of Morris Swett Library, Fires Center of Excellence.)

The camp for Indian scouts was usually pitched along the road from the trader's store to Quinette Crossing of Medicine Bluff Creek, a tributary of Cache Creek. Often, a dozen or more tepees indicated their presence, with their ponies tethered nearby. Their wives and children added a fascinating dimension to the early Fort Sill community. (Courtesy Morris Swett Library, Fires Center of Excellence.)

Indian scouts were indispensable in the planning of any military or police operation involving Native Americans. Recruited from among various tribes of Indian Territory, their ability to track, as well as their knowledge of the land, wildlife, and indigenous inhabitants, proved vitally important. Their uses included messengers, guides, escorts, and the pursuit of outlaws or Army deserters.

The Indian Trading Post was a branch store run by sutler John S. Evans and built near Cache Creek to the southeast of the fort. This view dates to about 1870. Colonel Grierson had outlawed all alcoholic beverages, so in place of beer or wine, Evans shipped in a lively tonic named Peruna, famed for its plum pudding flavor.

The Picket House is so named because it was constructed as a frame house with the outer boards standing upright, in the manner of a picket fence. Erected in 1869, it briefly served as quarters for officers, then as quarters for noncommissioned officers and their families. It is the oldest surviving structure at Fort Sill.

A row of picket houses ran along the east side of the quadrangle, parallel to the permanent company-grade officers' quarters (then under construction). This c. 1870 view shows Lt. and Mrs. A.S.B. Keyes and Capt. J.W. Walsh of the 10th Cavalry Regiment seated in front of the doorway to the house.

Officers' quarters were given an early priority, following the use of temporary picket houses and earlier forms of shelter like wall tents, pup tents, and lean-tos. Labor continued to consist chiefly of the enlisted ranks of the 10th Cavalry Regiment. Design and construction expertise were provided by civilian contractors recruited from Kansas. This view is looking toward the southeast around 1870.

The Old Post Quadrangle, or OPQ, is captured in this c. 1870 photograph taken facing northwest while it was under construction. Aside from a touring wagon on the left, there is an absence of laborers, perhaps due to inclement weather. Most of the buildings were sizable, requiring fantastic amounts of limestone, which was quarried and hauled from a mile away to the southeast. Timber and water were available a short distance to the north.

The cavalry stables provided shelter for the horses of the regiment. Each troop rode a distinctive color of horse. Situated to the west of the OPQ around 1870, these stables later accommodated the horses and mules of the Animal Transport Department of the Field Artillery School. The view is looking northwest. (Courtesy of Morris Swett Library, Fires Center of Excellence.)

The Stone Corral, seen in this c. 1950 view, was constructed in the summer of 1870 chiefly to safeguard the draft animals and their associated wagons that sustained early Fort Sill. Hostile Indians plagued the Army's supply of horses and mules, numbers of which changed hands. Loopholed for both defense and ventilation, it has been mistaken as the old fort by many visitors.

Indian villages were found throughout the region, some as near as the foot of Mount Scott. Tepees fashioned from buffalo hide and numerous lodgepoles provided shelter, warmed by a fire in the center. In the warmer months, the lower portion was elevated to provide occupants the benefit of cool, refreshing breezes. This camp belonged to Kiowa-Apache Chief Pacer around 1871.

Quakers were appointed as Indian agents early in the Grant administration. One famous such agent was Lawrie Tatum, who was threatened and bullied but eventually respected by soldiers, settlers, and tribesmen alike. He distributed gifts to his Indian charges and called upon the Army when it was needed to preserve order or aid in the return of captives.

William T. Sherman gained fame and promotion in the Civil War, becoming a lieutenant general in 1866 and a full general in 1869. He succeeded Ulysses S. Grant as commanding general of the US Army, remaining the highest-ranking general for 14 years (until 1883). He conducted a tour of inspection of frontier posts that turned perilous in May 1871.

The Sherman House was the quarters for the commanding officer and first lady of Fort Sill. It derives its name from General Sherman, who stayed there for several nights in May 1871. During his visit, the general had a dramatic confrontation with several Kiowa war chiefs on the front porch. A number were arrested and imprisoned for their part in the Warren Wagon Train Massacre, in which a hundred Indian warriors killed most of the teamsters of a small train of supply wagons.

The cavalry barracks on the west side of the quadrangle each accommodated a troop of enlisted soldiers, which might vary from about 30 to 70 troopers. The basement entry (dark twin doors) led to a prison prior to the construction of the guardhouse in 1875. Kiowa war chiefs were confined here following their arrest for participating in depredations in Texas in the spring of 1871. (Courtesy of Morris Swett Library, Fires Center of Excellence.)

Satanta, also called Set-tain-te or White Bear, was a signer of the Medicine Lodge Treaty in Kansas in 1867. He declared, "I love the land and the buffalo. . . . I love to roam over the prairies. . . . When I settle down I grow pale and die." He was a major figure in the cruel Warren Wagon Train Massacre.

Satank, or Sitting Bear, was a member of the Ten Bravest Warrior Society. When he was arrested, he resolved upon a warrior's death. As he was placed in an escort wagon destined for trial in Texas, he sang his death song. He managed to slip from his irons, stab a guard, and seize his gun. Soldiers' bullets struck him, and he died against a nearby tree on June 8, 1871.

Big Tree (Addo-ette) was the third Kiowa war chief arrested for his part in the Warren Wagon Train Massacre. He and Satanta were transported to trial in Texas, and although imperiled with the threat of hanging, he eventually returned to Indian Territory and helped his people keep the peace.

Stumbling Bear (Set-imkia) was a significant Kiowa war chief who was present at the Sherman House incident. He had earlier received the uniform of a major general as a token of his importance. When he was threatened with arrest, he shook off his blanket, which had been concealing his bow and arrow, and loosed an arrow at Sherman.

Kicking Bird was a peace chief of the Kiowas. When he saw his cousin Stumbling Bear take aim with his bow against General Sherman, he bumped his cousin's arm, causing him to miss. He knew that any harm coming to the great soldier chief Sherman would bring untold hardship upon his people. He died under a curse, according to the Kiowa—or by poison, according to an Army doctor, on May 3, 1875.

Lone Wolf (Gui-pah-go) was another prominent Kiowa chief involved in many raids into Texas. He played a prominent role in the Sherman House incident. He was a principal chief and was influential in affairs of both peace and war for many years.

A witness to the arrest and departure of the Kiowa chiefs was Caddo George Washington, chief of the Caddoes. He was an occasional supplier of intoxicating beverages, as well as firearms, to both the Kiowas and Comanches. During the Civil War, he led a company of scouts in the service of the South. He is pictured here around 1871.

The post hospital was built in the early 1870s for $10,000. There was a delay, however, as a controversy developed between the post surgeon and the commander, Col. B.H. Grierson. Location and size were at issue. Told the infirmary was too close to the cavalry stables, the colonel retorted, "who ever heard that it was unhealthy to be near stables?"

Band quarters were established in what has come to be known as Wichita House, erected in 1870 with a capacity for 20 soldiers. Colonel Grierson recruited men for the 10th Cavalry who were literate so that he could teach them music. The band played "The Girl I Left Behind Me" as troopers went forth on a mission and "When Johnny Comes Marching Home" upon their return.

Alice Grierson, wife of Col. B.H. Grierson, was known for her charming personality and caring nature. A courageous woman of the frontier, she also exerted a softening, refining, and compassionate influence at early day Fort Sill. She is pictured around 1872.

A stone blockhouse was constructed atop Signal Mountain in the summer of 1871. Soldiers assigned to this location communicated with a signaling station high in the cupola of the old post hospital. Any sign of hostile Indians was instantly communicated to the post commander. This view is from around 1889.

The Fort Sill Indian School was established in 1871, with Quaker Josiah Butler serving as the first teacher. After 1878, the approximate date of this view, the school became secularized, and in the years that followed its founding, many students attended. Prior to World War II, these consisted of Comanche, Kiowa, Arapaho, Caddo, Delaware, and Wichita, but later, students from tribes such as the Navajo predominated. It closed in 1980.

William H. Quinette was for many years the post trader at Fort Sill, providing most of the items eagerly sought after on the Western frontier. Born in 1853, he passed in 1937, and in his lifetime, he participated in the flourishing Fort Sill community, engaged in numerous business enterprises, including banking, and did much to promote the fort as well as early Lawton.

Col. (later general) Ranald Mackenzie was one of the most formidable military commanders of the Indian Wars. He was a key figure in the Red River War, directing three of the five columns of soldiers that participated in the war. He was also the Fort Sill commander who ordered the construction of the post chapel.

Buffalo hunters, such as the frontiersmen shown here, slaughtered huge numbers of American bison. Seeking hides at first and later the bones, they ruined the Indians' supply of not only meat but also shelter and numerous other components of the so-called "supermarket of the plains." Tribesmen vowed vengeance.

The Red River War (1874–1875) pitted formidable Indian warriors against converging columns of veteran bluecoats. Honors were about even, but victory went to the soldiers of the United States, who benefitted from superior logistics and strategy.

Ishi-tai was the Comanche medicine man who promised victory for Indian warriors in the Red River War, starting in 1874. Tribesmen yearned for the return of the buffalo and vowed to dispatch the greedy paleface hunters slaughtering the beasts that were essential to their tribal economy. His medicine was broken when he was knocked off his pony by a soldier's bullet at extreme range.

Quanah Parker, war chief of the Quohada Comanches, was the son of Chief Peta Nocona and a white captive, Cynthia Ann Parker. He fought in the Battle of Adobe Walls, and though unsuccessful during the Red River War, he proved an imposing leader. Astute, he eventually grew into the most powerful figure of his people in peace and in war. (Courtesy of Morris Swett Library, Fires Center of Excellence.)

Mow-Way, or Push Aside, was chief of the Kotchateka Comanches around 1873. A renowned leader, he warred against the whites when the Medicine Lodge Treaty promises of food and supplies were broken. He joined in many battles, including Adobe Walls and Palo Duro Canyon. Though he, too, surrendered, he is remembered as one of the great Comanche chiefs.

DISTRIBUTING SUPPLIES TO INDIANS.

WINTER LIFE ON THE PLAINS.—Drawn by P. Frenzeny.—[See Page 87.]

Reservation life was dismal for the proud, fierce Lords of the Plains as well as neighboring tribes around 1875. Government issues of food and other vital supplies were sometimes delayed. Even the beef issue, called *wo-haw* by the tribal members, was less satisfying than the supermarket of the plains, the amazing buffalo.

Big Bow grew up among the Quohada Comanches on the Staked Plains of Texas. He led his band until, like many, he surrendered to avoid the starvation of his people. He joined the US Army that same year (1875) and became a sergeant of scouts. In his life, he fought the Long Knives, Mexicans, cattle rustlers, Utes, and Navajo.

The Old Post Quadrangle included a spacious parade ground fronted by limestone barracks on the west and south sides, with quarters for officers on the east and north. This c. 1872 view is from the cupola on top of the hospital, which was later greatly expanded. Note the row of laundresses' quarters, the small buildings at far right. (Courtesy of Morris Swett Library, Fires Center of Excellence.)

Storehouses, warehouses, and other miscellaneous buildings were also built of limestone. The ordnance warehouse in the left foreground of this eastward-facing c. 1873 view is identified by two artillery caissons. The building with the chimney is likely the forge shop, while in the left distance is a view of Soapsuds Row, home and workplace of the post laundresses. (Courtesy of Morris Swett Library, Fires Center of Excellence.)

The guardhouse was completed by 1875. Among the first and certainly the most important detainees to be incarcerated were Kiowa war chiefs Big Tree, White Horse, and Woman's Heart. The threat of being locked away was a factor dissuading many a warrior, outlaw, or disgruntled soldier from serious acts of misbehavior.

The post chapel was completed in 1875. All new arrivals entering Fort Sill passed by this structure. The impression made by the chapel must have been a comfort and encouragement to many. Not only a place of worship, this was also where schoolchildren learned their "three Rs," soldiers got married, and many farewells were said.

The officers and their dependents who lived and served at Fort Sill belonged to the upper class. They did not mingle or mix socially with the enlisted soldiers and their families. Here, around 1875, an officer with his children peer from a balustrade. They are wearing casual yet stylish (for the frontier) clothing.

Army families were typified by that of Lt. Charles Cooper. His young daughter Forrestine, nicknamed "Cricket," made a lasting and profound impression upon the Fort Sill community in the early years. She wrote of her childhood memories and adventures growing up at Fort Sill and other Army posts in her book *Cricket, A Little Girl of the Old West*. This composite family image was taken on December 5, 1875.

Lt. Henry W. Lawton was so resourceful in his duties at early Fort Sill that he was styled the "Prince of Quartermasters." He served under Col. Ranald S. Mackenzie in the 4th Cavalry Regiment during his tour of duty in southwestern Indian Territory. He reverted to line command in subsequent years, winning promotion to general, but was killed in the Philippines in 1899.

Lt. Henry O. Flipper was the first black graduate of West Point. His record reflected expertise, especially in engineering, and linguistic talent. His tour of duty at Fort Sill, from 1877 to 1879, was distinguished by "Flipper's Ditch," his drainage system that successfully evacuated the stagnant pools of water responsible for harboring the insects that spread malarial fevers.

Horace P. Jones was the principal interpreter for Fort Sill, having earlier served in that capacity at Forts Arbuckle and Cobb. He married a Comanche woman and was assigned a residence just north of the post chapel. As master of hounds for many a hunt, his quarters were a favorite resort for many of the officers to smoke a cigar, swap news, and enjoy the dogs.

This watercolor painting is a bird's-eye view of the early days. A prominent quartermaster, Gen. Samuel A. Holabird, produced this rendering about 1877. Quarters for the officers, barracks for the enlisted, and supporting military structures were virtually complete and, interestingly, would form the most perfectly preserved Army post of the southern plains. The view is toward the west.

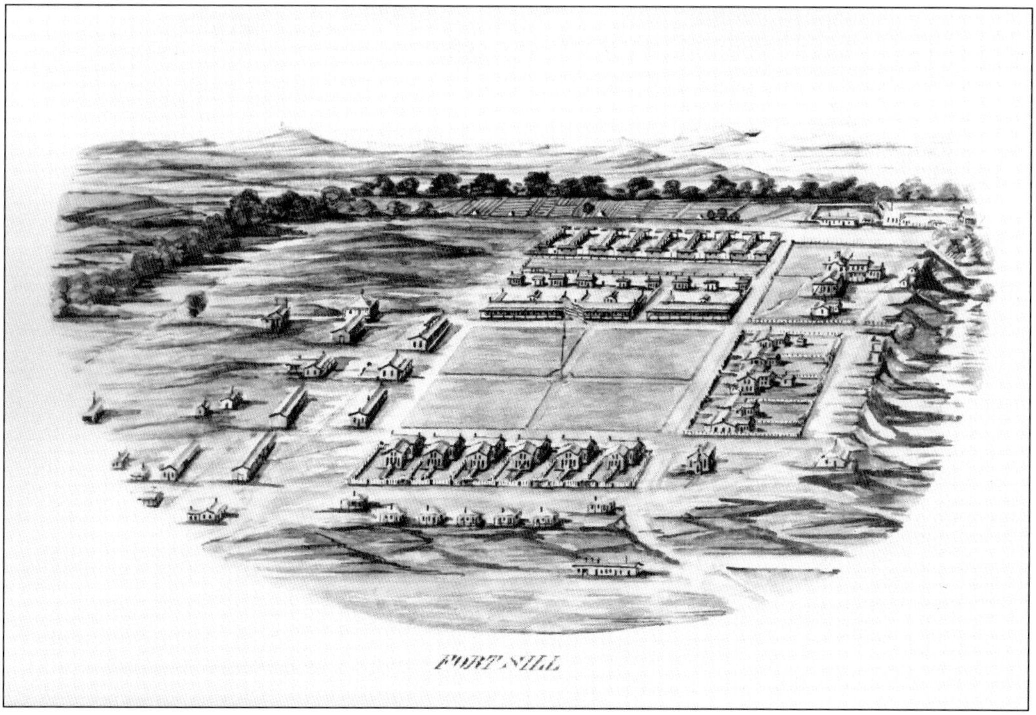

The northern row of officers' quarters was first to be completed. The white picket fence was utilitarian, keeping wandering animals from devouring flowerbeds and other embellishments painstakingly wrought by proprietary wives. Residential status was precarious, however, as sometimes occupants were ranked out—forced to move out by the arrival of a superior or senior officer. This view is from about 1880.

Field-grade officers' quarters were the most spacious at Fort Sill. This c. 1880 view of the north row includes the residences of captains, majors, lieutenant colonels, and the colonel himself. Residents included not only wives and children but also one or more live-in cooks, maids, and general-purpose servants.

Independence Day drew crowds from miles around. A social event of great magnitude, it featured baseball, horse and foot races, and even tug-of-war. The trader store and the Quinette house can be seen in the middle distance of this c. 1880 image, while the skyline includes Signal Mountain, Medicine Bluffs, and Mount Scott. (Courtesy of Morris Swett Library, Fires Center of Excellence.)

Surgeon and major Morse K. Taylor was one of the finest doctors to care for the early garrison. He ordered the construction of a springhouse to provide pure drinking water to soldiers and civilians of the early community. Located north of the hospital, it featured a stone trough inside the structure, which kept melons and fruit cool during the summertime. Completed in 1883, it was named for his wife, Ambrosia.

Ambrosia Taylor was the wife of the post doctor, Maj. Morse K. Taylor. Though an invalid, she was known for her kind and encouraging disposition. For many months, she cheered up the workers laboring on the construction of the springhouse ordered by her husband. She died in 1884, following its completion.

A permanent icehouse was established, an earlier one having been commandeered while yet unfinished for confining hostile Indian warriors at the conclusion of the Red River War in 1875. For many years, ice had been harvested from Medicine Bluff Creek, but during the 1880s, several mild winters resulted in a shortage. Following the completion of the water pumping plant north of the garrison area, the apparatus to make ice was acquired. This c. 1890 icehouse became a wonder to the Indians who inspected it, for it converted hot water into ice, even in the summertime. (Courtesy of Morris Swett Library, Fires Center of Excellence.)

Buffalo Soldiers of the 9th and 10th Cavalry were kept busy during the 1880s intercepting, arresting, and turning back illegal white immigrants who desired to occupy land in Indian Territory, now known as Oklahoma. Few confrontations were resisted; these horse soldiers, seen here around 1885, were known for their valor and skill.

Lt. Hugh L. Scott arrived at Fort Sill in 1889. An expert in frontier warfare, he also excelled in diplomacy. One favorable trait he possessed was his expertise in Indian sign language. He cultivated friends among the tribal warriors and leaders, which stood him in good stead during some troubles in the following years.

The children of Lieutenant Scott had some great times at Fort Sill, including their share of mischief. This c. 1890 photograph shows some innocent fun as they are splashed with a water hose at the hands of 7th Cavalry lieutenant S.R.H. "Tommy" Tompkins.

Picnics and outings, such as this one in the 1890s, whether by horse or carriage, were engaged in by officers, their wives and sweethearts, and occasional visitors. Weekends provided a welcome opportunity to socialize and relax. The surrounding countryside was picturesque and offered good hunting, too.

Masquerades and soirees afforded relief from hard and sometimes dangerous duty and were treasured by the women of the garrison. In this c. 1890 scene, the men have dressed like women and the women like men. Hilarious hijinks no doubt followed.

This panorama shows cavalrymen lined up in front of William Quinette's store and home. Unsettled conditions on the northern plains during the early 1890s involving the Ghost Dance threatened to spread southward. Additional contingents of cavalrymen were ordered to Forts Sill and Reno.

A mounted salute is rendered from these superb horsemen of Troops E, F, H, and K of the 7th Cavalry Regiment and Troops D and L of the 5th Cavalry Regiment. Their M1860 sabers are presented in front of their faces upon the word of command. Officers' quarters can be seen in the distance.

The Ghost Dance came to the Comanches, Cheyenne, and Arapahoe in 1891. Other tribesmen joined in hopes that the old days might return, with plentiful buffalo and the pleasure and independence of their former lifestyle. Dances such as this one, three years later, were believed to be essential in making the necessary medicine.

Tragedy was averted on the southern plains by men such as Lt. H.L. Scott and famed Indian scout I-See-O (Plenty Fires). By sign language, soldier and warrior agreed that there was no medicine in this dance and that better conditions could be brought about through trust and cooperation. I-See-O later became senior sergeant of Troop L, 7th Cavalry.

This 1895 fire drill was carried out along the approaches to the officers' quarters of the north row. Cavalrymen in ranks observed the admonitions of their instructors. Demanding exertions included the procedures of the veteran firemen opposite each of the dormers on the roof of the quarters under mock duress.

The old post chapel was used for a variety of purposes. In addition to raising morale and providing comfort in the way of religious services, the chapel honored the fallen and those many felled by sickness, and was the scene of many marriages. In addition, it offered a convenient venue for the education of children (as well as soldiers), like those pictured in this c. 1896 photograph. For many years, it acted as the social center of the Fort Sill community, with soirees, dances, and patriotic and seasonal events celebrated here.

Geronimo, famous leader of Apache resistance, led his band of Chiricahuas in defiance of efforts to confine them to a reservation with minimal subsistence. He surrendered to US forces for the last time in 1886. As partial consolation, the Army provided him and Chief Naiche a new pair of cowboy boots.

After eight years of incarceration in Alabama and Florida, Geronimo and his people were ordered to Fort Sill, where they remained for many years as prisoners of war. However, they were provided housing, livestock, and the rudiments of an improved standard of living. Geronimo's garden, pictured around 1895, produced useful supplements to issued foodstuffs.

Like many Fort Sill Apaches, Geronimo used his skill as a horseman to successfully manage livestock on their reservation. Contrary to legend, Geronimo lived peacefully and did not engage local cavalrymen, nor did he attempt to elude them by jumping his horse over any cliffs. He is seen here about 1896.

Geronimo (left) was a magnificent warrior, but one must remember that it was Naiche (right), second son of the great Cochise, who was the chief of the Chiricahuas. Here they pose together around 1896, suggesting that they continued as partners in peace as they had been in war. Indeed, they led their people with signal success.

Geronimo (originally named Go-Yah-kla, One Who Yawns) was not a chief but an awesome medicine man and a superb leader in war. He mystified cavalrymen with his ability to elude them while at the same time finding sustenance for his band. Relegated to a minor role by military authorities, he enlisted as a scout, serving as Private Geronimo in the late 1890s.

Several members of Company E, 10th Infantry Regiment, were comically inclined. These soldiers appear in a scene from 1896 at Fort Sill. Some sport civilian attire, some military, but they all speak to a high sense of humor.

Various social pastimes relieved the boredom of frontier military life. Parlor games sometimes led to romance and marriage. In chaplain Maj. Brant C. Hammond's quarters, from left to right, his daughter, Blanche Hammond, William H. Quinette (the post trader), Grace, and a brother, Gerold, enjoyed such games and formed lasting ties. Not long after this image was captured around 1900, Blanche married Quinette.

The old post hospital was a large structure, seen here looking toward the south around 1900. Although the post commander believed that even 12 beds were excessive, from the time of its completion, it featured 50, and more were soon added by means of wings and reorganization. Throughout the Indian Wars, the hospital saved numerous lives through the expertise of its medical personnel and their insistence on sanitation.

Two

A New Mission, A New City

Pres. William McKinley proclaimed the opening of the Indian reservations (Kiowas, Comanches, Kiowa-Apaches, Wichitas, and Caddoes) to homesteaders on July 4, 1901, by lottery. Registration was held at Fort Sill in the southern district and at Fort Reno in the northern district from July 10 to 26. Fort Sill, comprising 45,000 acres, was exempt. A townsite five miles south was planned, and Lawton (named for Gen. Henry W. Lawton) sprang up overnight as a boomtown tent city on August 6.

Beginning in 1902, individual batteries of artillery, starting with the 29th Field Artillery Battery, began to arrive for training at Fort Sill. Provisional artillery regiments were formed. The cannoneers lived in tents opposite the trader's store until quarters became available.

By 1907, the artillery mission was rapidly displacing the cavalry's peacekeeping mission. Indeed, growth and modernization threatened to bring down and replace the original limestone structures. These historic buildings, large and small, were saved in 1908 by the order of Secretary of War William H. Taft, who valued their romantic historical associations.

At first, conditions were primitive, as in a regimental tent camp. The original School of Fire was a very small and modest building. Capt. Dan T. Moore was assigned as the first commandant. Artillery officers were taught at least the rudiments of their trade. New Post sprang up a short distance to the west of the Old Post. New buildings for administration and classroom instruction were erected, as well as barracks for the enlisted and quarters for the officers.

In 1916, the School of Fire for Field Artillery was closed. American forces of all arms were shifted to the Mexican border to participate in the Pershing expedition. However, in 1917, with American entry into World War I, the School of Fire reopened in earnest. Col. (later major general) William J. Snow arrived as commandant on July 27. Soon he was named the first chief of field artillery.

Other developments included the creation of the Wichita Mountains Wildlife Refuge, the first of its kind, just west of Fort Sill in 1901. Fifteen American bison, commonly called buffalo, were reintroduced into the refuge from New York. The passing of an age seemed signaled by the passing of Geronimo in 1909 and Quanah Parker in 1911. The Apache prisoners of war were permitted to return to New Mexico in 1913; the 87 who remained thereafter became known as the Fort Sill Apaches.

Lawton was born on August 6, 1901. Less than a month later, the first example of prefabricated housing arrived, as seen in this view. The prairie city counted over 25,000 citizens within a few weeks. The main street was given the curious name of Goo-Goo Avenue, which ran east-to-west. The Santa Fe Railroad reached Lawton on September 25 and the Frisco line shortly afterward. This photograph dates to September 1, 1901.

The Apache prisoners of war included numerous children. These boys were issued white shirts and striped, bib-front trousers, plus shoes to wear. Their hair was cut, but there were no hats or caps available in their size. In this c. 1905 view, they have just exited the Apache Mission School.

Apache girls were also expected to learn the White Man's Road. Anna Vos taught the girls how to peel apples and prepare meals as part of domestic science at the Apache Mission School in the early 1900s. From left to right are Minnie Dee, Isabel Enjady, Irene Gooday, Eloise Perico, and Anna Vos.

A fine example of an Apache girl was Eliza Koonie. She shared a dual culture, cherishing her Native American ways and values while at the same time not only striving but thriving in the white man's world. In this c. 1905 view, she holds her prized doll.

Geronimo was a celebrity people came to see from miles around. He sold souvenirs of himself, including portrait postcards. He made money by appearing in Wild West shows, parades, and various appearances. He also got into occasional mischief, was confined in the old guardhouse on a few occasions, and had to chop firewood before his breakfast the next morning. These stints gave rise to the legend that he was held for years in a cell in the basement, which is not true.

Comanche chief Quanah Parker adapted well and was especially successful in business with Texas cattlemen, sharing his financial success with many of his fellow Comanches. Appointed judge over his people's legal affairs, he performed his duties with integrity. He owned an elegant home, kept several wives, and enjoyed going into the bustling city of Lawton in his own four-horse coach. He was a man of many talents, even starring in early movies. This c. 1908 image captures some of his personality.

The Star House was the home of Quanah Parker, built before the turn of the 20th century. It derived its name from the fact that the roof was decorated with large, white, five-pointed stars. Quanah loved to entertain important, high-ranking Army officers and declared that he was not intimidated by anyone, as his house had more stars than they wore upon their shoulders.

The chaplain's quarters are the first residence along east officers' row, just south of the chapel, in this view from 1910. When marriageable daughters were in residence, their desire for socials led to some lively events. Hops, or dances, were popular means by which members of the post became acquainted, although enlisted men were always kept separate from officers. The chaplain was usually involved, as the chapel was the principal locale for these events.

The old post chapel was the rendezvous for band practice. Military music brightened many a dreary day, particularly in the early years of the post. Performances with so many musical instruments and players were commonly enjoyed on the spacious parade ground, at one time from a nearby gazebo. This 1913 image recalls the patriotic marches of John Philip Sousa as well as contemporary favorites ranging from ragtime to Western ballads.

A new guardhouse was constructed in the New Post area, as seen here in 1911, to replace the aging structure from the Indian Wars. It incorporated several modern features: all-steel doors for the inmates' cells, electrical wiring for the lighting, and of course, plumbing.

Capt. Dan T. Moore was appointed the first commandant of the School of Fire for Field Artillery. He had served as an observer for the War Department in 1908 and 1909, studying and comparing European artillery methods and materiel. He examined the British, Dutch, Austrian, and German armies and implemented a successful plan to launch a competitive American training program, albeit on a small scale, at Fort Sill in 1911.

The first School of Fire for Field Artillery was conducted in this small building. It was the headquarters of Captain Moore, assisted by his secretary, Lt. Ralph McT. Pennell, and Sgt. Maj. Lynn Boggs. In 1911, the classroom accommodated its first students, 14 captains and 22 noncommissioned officers. This view dates to about 1910.

The War Department assigned the field artillery mission to Fort Sill. Modernization required great development and expansion. New Post construction provided large, spacious, and comparatively luxurious quarters for officers assigned to the post. This view looks toward the northwest around 1914.

This bird's-eye view of the OPQ was taken about 1913 and features the chapel in the foreground, complete with a sheltered woodpile. The chaplain's quarters are immediately to the left, and a vacant lot is just to the right, or west. A senior officer's quarters to the right appear with a wing addition, also built of limestone.

A higher aerial view of Fort Sill looks to the west about 1913. The Old Post Quadrangle is easily identifiable, while some of the New Post construction can be discerned near the top of the image. A railroad runs along the lower edge.

The 5th Field Artillery Band plays rousingly as the national colors are raised upon the occasion of the regiment's arrival at Fort Sill on February 10, 1912. New Post is in operation; the headquarters were placed in Building 1955 on Randolph Road. This was an imposing building opposite the Administration Building.

Native Americans, especially the Fort Sill Apaches, formed their own baseball team to play against the soldiers, giving them competition at their own game. Seen in 1913, the Fort Sill Indians wore their baseball uniforms with pride. Their equipment was of the latest standard, evidenced by the gloves and bats in the foreground.

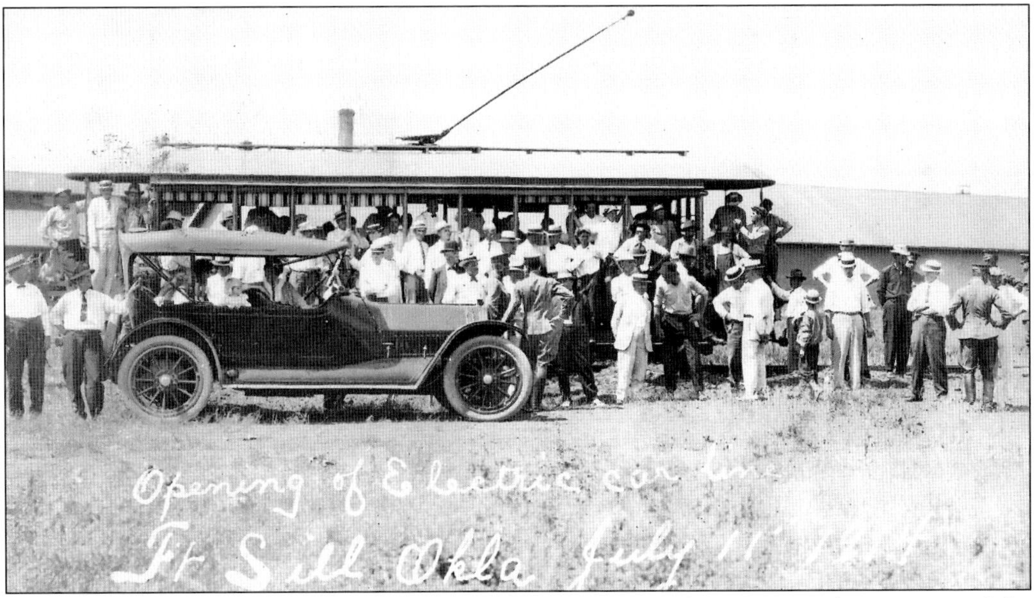

As war clouds gathered in Europe, Fort Sill stepped up its modernization. The opening of the electric trolley car took place on July 11, 1914, as seen here. A dignitary attended with his Model T touring car (left). This postcard image cost 1¢ to mail across the country.

This 1917 image displays a more detailed view of the trolley providing transportation from Lawton to Fort Sill. Motorman (driver) Fred Russell can be seen on the step next to conductor Charlie Bevis, standing on the ground. A soldier is seated behind Russell, and a civilian passenger is inside the trolley. A cowcatcher protrudes below the sign on the front reading "Lawton–Fort Sill Inter-Urban 1."

Three

Camp Doniphan and Over There

The United States declared war on Germany in April 1917. Immediately, the need arose for training camps to prepare an army capable of joining combat in Europe and securing victory by force of arms.

At first, the suggestion of Fort Sill as a training camp was rejected due to a perceived shortage of water for the thousands of anticipated trainees. However, Lawton civic leaders, including W.H. Quinette, with the support of townsfolk, pledged five million gallons of water daily for the post. The offer was accepted. The cantonment was named Camp Doniphan, recalling a hero of the Mexican-American War, Col. Alexander W. Doniphan.

The School of Musketry was greatly expanded, as was the School of Field Artillery and other military ventures. Camp Doniphan was built to the west of New Post and sprawled southwards. The camp consisted of 1,200 acres in the shape of a horseshoe opening to the east. In the summer of 1917, it welcomed elements of the 36th Division (Oklahoma National Guard). In September, the 35th Division (Kansas and Missouri National Guard) arrived and trained for six months.

One battery commander of the 129th Field Artillery Regiment was destined for greatness—Capt. Harry S. Truman of Missouri later became the 33rd president of the United States. After the departure of the doughboys, Camp Doniphan became a field artillery brigade training center commanded by Brig. Gen. Edmund L. Gruber, celebrated composer of the popular song "The Caissons Go Rolling Along."

To implement such ambitious programs of military training, Brig. Gen. Montgomery M. Macomb was recalled from retirement and given command of Fort Sill. He worked together with Col. (later major general) William J. Snow and others to achieve great results.

Fort Sill made remarkable contributions to victory in World War I. The infantry and artillery men trained at Camp Doniphan participated in victories on the western front. Aerial observers directed artillery fire, a decisive element in modern war. And Native Americans distinguished themselves in combat, terrifying enemies already intimidated by stories of their ferocity. A handful of tribesmen pioneered a new specialty, code talking, utilizing their native languages to secure vital communications.

During the war, Camp Doniphan trained over 50,000 American soldiers. In the years of peace that followed, the cantonment continued in use during the summertime by units of the Oklahoma National Guard.

Camp Doniphan incorporated the artillerymen undergoing training in the School of Fire, adding to the regular students the batteries forming up in the National Guards of Oklahoma, Kansas, and Missouri. The horse was still essential in moving guns and caissons to mass fire on the battlefield, even in World War I.

The officer on horseback supervises his cannoneers as they load ammunition designated by command. These M1902 three-inch field guns were common until the arrival of the famous M1897 "French 75s." American artillery materiel was in short supply, so when these artillerymen deployed to France, they used borrowed French field guns and howitzers for the most part.

Camp Doniphan is shown from the air in this c. 1918 photograph, probably taken from a Curtiss JN-4, known as a "Jenny." The Wichita Mountains limited the growth of the tent encampment westward, so expansion developed southward, toward the city of Lawton.

Lt. (later captain) Harry S. Truman was a battery commander of the 129th Field Artillery Regiment at Camp Doniphan in the fall of 1917. He loved practical jokes and wrote many letters recalling them to his wife, who waited for him at home in Missouri, later published in the book *Dear Bess*. In 1945, he became president of the United States.

While Camp Doniphan trained soldiers going "over there," into the cockpit of battle in Europe, Old Post buildings were well maintained and likewise supported soldier readiness. In this scene from around 1918, two Fort Sill soldiers wearing Montana hats discuss affairs while standing on the porch of the old cavalry barracks.

Col. (later major general) William J. Snow served as post commander and was the first chief of field artillery. He developed the School of Fire for Field Artillery and expanded its program from July to December 1917. He overcame immense logistical difficulties and fiscal challenges and made a substantial contribution to America's victory in World War I. This portrait is from 1918.

In addition to the tents accommodating the soldiers in training, wooden buildings were erected to house kitchens and infirmaries and to maintain and safeguard heavy equipment. Mechanization was apparent, from Model Ts to liberty trucks and artillery tractors, as seen here around 1918.

Soldiers relaxed after duty hours. By 1918, the enlisted men's quarters were the pride of Fort Sill. Planned 11 years previously by the chief of staff of the Army, Maj. Gen. Franklin Bell, the post had truly become, in many respects, the show place for the Army.

Pvt. Antone "Tony" Soukup poses with his Ford Model T touring car and his faithful camera in 1918 during one of his off-duty moments. He probably took photographs of his buddies as they trained and during free time. Camp Doniphan offered the attractions of nearby Lawton as well as hunting opportunities in the adjacent Wichita Mountains.

Soldiers continued to ride the trolley into Lawton whenever opportunity presented itself. The prospects of cafés, saloons, sightseeing, and meeting women were all powerful inducements to visit the city, the population of which had declined a few years earlier but was once more over 20,000. The time frame of this image is 1917–1921.

Gen. John J. "Blackjack" Pershing (left) led America to victory in World War I. Here, he commends and congratulates another hero, Sgt. I-See-O. His name means "Plenty Fires," and he was senior sergeant of Indian scouts during the 1890s. By command directive, he was never to be reduced or retired. This photograph was taken on January 8, 1922.

The Liberty Theatre was a great boost to the soldiers' morale, especially after arduous study in the classroom and trying service in the field. In this view from 1923, some war trophies in the form of captured German cannons enhance the approaches. These pieces were later donated to the Fort Sill Museum.

Off-duty hours at Fort Sill were sometimes lively affairs, as seen in this view of a pair of pugnacious pugilists. This c. 1924 view shows Privates Larosa (left) and Ramos as they spar to determine who will be champ.

The post hospital was enlarged with additional wings and was assigned the use of smaller adjacent buildings during the World War I era. While the original structure was basically unaltered, the increased space, pictured around 1925, was used for the accommodation of medical personnel, many more beds for patients, examining rooms with the latest medical apparatus, and facilities for operations as well as rehabilitation.

The original Snow Hall perished in a calamitous fire on August 8, 1929. The late 1920s witnessed a suspicious number of conflagrations on the post. Eventually, the arsonists were apprehended; for the most part, they were members of the fire department and associated security personnel.

In 1925, Pres. Calvin Coolidge invited Native American soldiers to the White House in recognition of their service and valor. In this scene are, from left to right, George Hunt, Guy Quetone, Taune-Quoot (Kiowa), Albert Attocknie (Comanche), President Coolidge, I-See-O, Ahpeahtone (Kiowa), Pa-Que-opeth (Comanche), and Oti-Poby (Comanche).

Craterville Park was a remarkable diversion for the soldiers and civilians of the Fort Sill–Lawton community. Nestled along the southern fringe of the Wichita Mountains, it featured an impressive fairground, complete with displays and concessions, pageants, and a variety of wholesome recreations. This view is dated 1926.

An Indian war dance mesmerizes spectators in this scene from Craterville Park in 1928. Local soldiers and civilians found it popular, and tourists flocked to enjoy the fun and frolic from as far away as Oklahoma City and northern Texas.

Boxing remained a favorite pastime for many soldiers, both as a participatory and as a spectator sport. In 1939, the 1st Field Artillery Regiment parades its boxing squad before the camera, along with those of the Oklahoma State Junior Amateur Athletic Union, in front of one of the buildings of Fort Sill.

Four

Cradle of Army Aviation

Combat aviation was born at Fort Sill in 1915. The 1st Aero Squadron's eight Curtiss JN-2 Jennies made their first flights in August commanded by Capt. Benjamin D. Foulois. Soon, aerial photography in support of artillery was underway. The squadron flew south on November 19 to support operations in the Pershing expedition against Mexico's revolutionary Pancho Villa.

In August 1917, a permanent airstrip was established named Henry Post Army Airfield after a pilot killed in an accident in California. Wooden hangars and auxiliary buildings were erected. Military aircraft were gathered, both airplanes and balloons, and a training program was inaugurated to prepare aircrew for observation duties in support of field artillery.

The end of World War I witnessed the growth of aviation activities at Fort Sill. In the years that followed, despite occasional setbacks involving accidents and fires, progress continued. Balloons were predominant. Sausage-shaped "captured" balloons were reinforced with spherical "free" balloons as refinements improved in aerial observation. In 1937, self-propelled balloons were devised to expedite their arrival at a designated position, after which the motor was removed and a gondola (basket) with two aircrew was attached.

An all-metal balloon hangar was relocated to Fort Sill from Moffitt Field, California, in 1934. Many dirigibles were used in training artillery observers while utilizing this hangar. It remained in use until 1941.

By 1940, most aerial spotting for the artillery shifted to fixed-wing aircraft. The Army Air Corps turned Post Field over to the Field Artillery School. It immediately started training forward observers with Grasshoppers, the light utility airplanes used in World War II. Great successes were achieved by these means, and in the Korean conflict that followed, improved aircraft, Bird Dogs, continued in similar duties.

In the 1960s, aerial observation was supplemented by forward air control, by which helicopters utilized target-marking rockets, and by aerial field artillery: helicopters using air-to-ground munitions.

Helicopters in all sizes and shapes have symbolized much of the modern history of Fort Sill. Although the Army Aviation School transferred to Fort Rucker, Alabama, in 1954, aviation has continued as an integral part of the artillery team.

Vastly improved aircraft, whether fixed wing or rotary, have continued to be employed at Fort Sill. Military aviation remains indispensable. And Henry Post Army Airfield is the oldest continually operating airfield in the United States.

The 1st Aero Squadron made history when it assembled at Fort Sill in the summer of 1915. Army aircraft commenced operations in squadron strength. Here, a crowd examines one of the Curtiss JN-4 Jennies prior to a flight from the airstrip. Aircraft were uncrated and assembled on the Parade Ground.

Disaster occurred when a hydrogen-filled balloon caught fire due to a spark of static electricity on April 2, 1918; the terrifying explosion killed six soldiers. Thirty more were injured as they were holding on to the guide ropes. Several returned to pull the balloon away from nearby wooden barracks.

Dozens of soldiers were assigned on a rotating basis to the launch and retrieval of military balloons. With careful handling and expert timing, the lighter-than-air balloons, with an aircrew of one or two seasoned observers, were successfully launched aloft and retrieved hours later.

Sausage-shaped balloons were the style predominantly used by American military observers on the western front. At an altitude of 4,000 feet, they were usually immune to small-arms fire from the ground. However, when incendiary bullets and aerial rockets were employed against them, they became an endangered species around 1918.

The 1st Balloon Company soldiers can be seen walking a sausage-style observation balloon into its wooden hangar at Post Field, Fort Sill, around 1929, long after the Great War was over.

The autogyro was an experimental aircraft of the 1930s. Fort Sill investigated its potential as an observation platform serving field artillery. It was unsuccessful due to its inability to hover, but led eventually to fruitful developments as helicopters emerged. This view dates to about 1935.

Five

The Challenge of World War II and Korea

On December 13, 1930, Secretary of War Patrick J. Hurley designated Fort Sill the permanent home of field artillery. In the years that followed, Gen. Leslie J. McNair and others brilliantly reorganized and refined the branch of service. Talented American officers established the Fire Direction Center (1932–1934) to centralize computer firing data in the battalion. This system surpassed any other in the world. Insistence by ranking officers led to the development of ENIAC, the world's first computer, as a means of acquiring accurate firing data.

In 1941, Fort Sill began training promising individuals for officer duties. The Officer Candidate School (OCS) produced over 26,000 second lieutenants of field artillery by December 1946. Many thousand enlisted personnel were processed through the Artillery Replacement Center.

Massing of fire was achieved on so many battlefields that Gen. George S. Patton declared once, addressing artillerymen, "I don't have to tell you who won the war. You know you did!"

During the later years of World War II, camps were instituted with prisoners of two sorts. Some were civilians: those of Japanese ancestry who were suspected of disloyalty. Secondly were German and Italian prisoners of war from the successful campaign in North Africa. These camps were situated approximately where Camp Doniphan had been.

Native Americans responded to America's call to arms. Code talkers, utilizing tribal languages, proved to be of great value. The Army recruited Comanches from their homes not far from Fort Sill. Over a dozen of these brave men earned combat distinction and left a proud legacy.

As the nuclear age dawned, Fort Sill developed artillery that employed either conventional or nuclear projectiles. The original 280-millimeter gun, "Atomic Annie," fired its epic round at Frenchman's Flat, Nevada. Its crew trained at Fort Sill. During the late 1950s, some batteries deployed to distant outposts of the Army, including Western Europe.

War in Korea again tested the capabilities of American artillery. Despite setbacks and even retreats, US firepower held the line and denied victory to the enemy. South Korea has enjoyed democratic freedom to this day.

The Field Artillery School Administration Building was completed and occupied on April 18, 1935, and is shown around 1943. The first permanent home of the Field Artillery School, it was later named McNair Hall after Lt. Gen. Leslie J. McNair. He did much to reorganize and modernize American artillery, and was killed in a bombing attack near Saint-Lô, France, during World War II. (Courtesy of Morris Swett Library, Fires Center of Excellence.)

The Old Post Guardhouse was commandeered and designated the Fort Sill Museum in 1934. The collection grew as Lt. (later colonel) Harry Larter traveled throughout the states gathering cannons and artillery artifacts while at the same time safeguarding Native American treasures, including the weapons and personal effects of famous tribesmen like Quanah Parker and Geronimo. This view dates to 1943. (Courtesy of Morris Swett Library, Fires Center of Excellence.)

Equestrian skills continued to be admired long after the cavalry days had ended. In this scene from around 1935, Lieutenant Coverdale jumps his horse over the hurdles at Rucker Park, a favorite training area for perfecting horsemanship.

The Fort Sill Hunt was an organization consisting primarily of military officers who enjoyed the centuries-old traditions of the hunt. More than a fox was at stake, for they competed in international equestrian contests, proving their prowess by winning medals in the 1932 Olympics and trophies from a 1935 meet in Mexico.

The quick-fire 2.95-inch mountain gun was a lightweight and rugged British weapon designed for rapid deployment in colonial service. The US Army purchased a dozen of these for use in the Philippine Islands, including action with the Philippine scouts in the early months of World War II. This c. 1935 view shows the huge cloud of smoke after discharge.

A column of pack mules and "redlegs" (as members of the field artillery were known) surmount rugged terrain as they undergo training in the mountains near Fort Sill in 1942. The 4th Field Artillery Regiment used the Pack 75, a lightweight, portable howitzer with a respectable punch. Mule-borne artillery is commemorated to this day at Fort Sill.

Artillery trainees learned to quickly unload, assemble, and prepare the Pack 75 for firing. Older models, such as the one seen here, featured wooden spoked wheels reminiscent of World War I. Most that saw action in World War II had pneumatic tires, were capable of rapid assembly and disassembly, and could be transported by pack animal or aircraft.

Artillery training in World War II was thorough and exhausting. The replacement center invested many months in preparing artillerymen for any contingency on the battlefield. The M2 155-millimeter "Long Tom" threw a 100-pound shell at some of the deepest of Fort Sill's firing ranges. This scene is from 1943.

Veteran aerial forward observer Col. William W. Ford (left) shakes hands with a fellow officer in 1946. He commanded the Army Ground Forces Air Training School at Fort Sill. Ford's aircraft is a Piper L-4 Grasshopper.

Light utility aircraft operated from Henry Post Army Airfield during World War II. This Cessna LC-126 has been secured between flights with its wheels chocked and the tips of its wings tethered. It had a capacity of one pilot and five passengers. Behind it is an L-4 Grasshopper observation and liaison aircraft. The timeframe is around 1950.

During the Korean War, artillerymen deployed from Fort Sill were in great demand. In this scene from July 19, 1950, Sgt. Henry Feinberg of Boston, Massachusetts, section chief of a 155-millimeter M114 howitzer battery, supervises fire upon North Korean soldiers. Crewmen dubbed this model of howitzer "the Pig."

Six

The Cold War Years

After 1945, the world was largely divided into two armed camps. The United States led the free world, promoting democratic institutions that safeguarded human rights. The Soviet Union led those countries that subscribed to communist ideals and ideology.

The result was a protracted stalemate, with distrust and antipathy between the two parties. Fort Sill received government appropriations that enabled it to maintain its status and, in some respects, surpass its previous achievements. On November 1, 1946, it was reorganized as the US Artillery Center. New buildings arose for academic instruction, facilities were enlarged for training, and programs were initiated for weapons testing and development. The post hospital was expanded to include 250 beds and state-of-the-art clinics, all staffed with skilled medical personnel.

A branch was established at Fort Bliss, Texas, called the Antiaircraft and Guided Missile School. The twin branches of artillery (field artillery and air defense) developed separately for over 60 years.

In 1954, postwar construction provided a new academic headquarters and classroom building. Features included a large auditorium and a modern library named for the noncommissioned officer who had done so much to develop library science on post during the 1930s, M.Sgt. Morris Swett. The building was christened after the first chief of field artillery, Maj. Gen. William J. Snow (an earlier building had burned in 1929). The artillery center headquarters remained McNair Hall.

During the 1950s and 1960s, new technologies were exploited. Atomic artillery became a reality, as tactical projectiles were provided for tube artillery "just in case they were needed." Atomic Annie, a 280-millimeter nuclear-capable cannon, demonstrated its potential during those years.

Rockets and missiles came of age, as testified by such weapons as Honest John, Corporal, Sergeant, Pershing, and others. Each succeeding weapon system had a greater deterrent potential. Tube artillery, especially self-propelled, became ever more mobile and lethal.

During the Vietnam era, helicopter pads proliferated at Fort Sill. Dozens of whirlybirds, from single-seat trainers and utility rotors to combat, liaison, and transport types, undertook the training of crews.

The Cold War ended with the collapse of the Soviet Union in 1991, as free elections ousted communist regimes throughout Eastern Europe. Fort Sill had played a vital role in safeguarding democracy and promoting freedom worldwide.

This Honest John rocket, part of a firing demonstration, lifts off from its mobile launcher truck mount around 1959. It was the Army's first nuclear-capable surface-to-surface rocket. It had an operational range of over 15 miles, with an alternate warhead of 15,000 pounds.

Firepower demonstrations have always been popular attractions for soldiers and civilians alike. In this 1960 demo, onlookers thrill to see an Honest John rocket begin its flight. Crowded on the bleachers of Mow-Way House, visitors from far and near attended the exciting event.

This Beechcraft L-23 Seminole rests between flights at Henry Post Army Airfield around 1960. It was a light utility aircraft produced from 1952 to 1963. Over 283 were built. Many performed surveillance missions, remaining in service for over 40 years, including the Vietnam era.

Helicopter crews who trained at Fort Sill saw extensive service during Vietnam. The Boeing CH-47 Chinook delivered howitzers, munitions, and other supplies throughout the conflict and for many years afterwards. This c. 1969 view is from an in-theater operation.

The Sikorsky CH-54 Tarhe, also known as the Skycrane, was a twin-engine heavy-lift-capable helicopter. Seen here about 1970, its crew consisted of a pilot, a copilot, and either an engineer or a rear-facing observer. It normally carried up to five passengers and a payload of over 5,000 pounds.

First Sgt. Pascal C. Poolaw Sr. won the distinction of becoming America's most decorated Native American soldier. A full-blooded Kiowa, Poolaw won a battlefield commission in World War II, resumed his military career in Korea, and gave his life in combat during Vietnam. He earned four Silver Stars, five Bronze Stars, and three Purple Hearts among 42 military medals and citations. This view of him is from 1967.

This M198 155-millimeter howitzer is being fired at near-maximum elevation at a Fort Sill firing range around 1972. It featured a split trail and was towed into firing position. It replaced the veteran M114 155-millimeter howitzer in the early 1970s. Used extensively by both the Army and the Marines, it can fire up to 14 miles with a sustained rate of fire of two rounds per minute. (Courtesy of US Army Artillery Museum.)

Lt. Gen. David C. Ott made significant contributions to the development of modern American artillery. This c. 1976 view portrays him when he was a major general at Fort Sill. In addition to the roles of chief of field artillery, commandant of the Field Artillery School, and commanding general of the Field Artillery Center, he developed the fire support team, counterfire, and other advances. (Courtesy of Morris Swett Library, Fires Center of Excellence.)

The Medical Assistance (MAST) program at Fort Sill provided quick-response helicopters to aid civilians or military personnel in need of immediate response. This scene from about 1982 demonstrates how the injured were rushed to medical facilities in liaison with the Oklahoma Highway Patrol.

Maj. Gen. Charles R. Reynolds (1877–1961) of the Army Medical Corps was the surgeon general from 1933 to 1939. A superb clinical surgeon, he taught advanced medical procedures and led by example, being cited for heroism as he cared for wounded soldiers in combat. His name was selected for memorialization on the post's principal healthcare facility. (Courtesy of Reynolds Army Health Clinic Public Affairs Office.)

The cantonment hospital at Fort Sill was an expedient measure created in 1941 as the Army rapidly expanded to meet the challenge of global war. Sometimes referred to as the "annex hospital," it was located near Gate 2 and served as a place of recovery until Building 4700 was constructed in 1965. (Courtesy of US Army Artillery Museum.)

In 1965, Reynolds Army Hospital was dedicated and opened at Fort Sill. It operated 250 beds, replacing the two medical facilities up to that time: the cantonment hospital on the east side of the post and Taylor Hall. It was named for Maj. Gen. Charles R. Reynolds. (Courtesy of Reynolds Army Health Clinic Public Affairs Office.)

Reynolds Army Hospital and related buildings can be readily identified in this c. 1989 aerial view. In addition to soldiers in training or part of the garrison, other patients, such as dependents, also received treatment. All manner of services were rendered, from birth deliveries to dental and optical services as well as more serious surgeries. (Courtesy of US Army Artillery Museum.)

In 1989, a greatly enlarged medical facility took the name once more of Major General Reynolds. Its 157 beds could be expanded to 247 upon mobilization. Phase two added a significant ancillary support building, resulting in the building's rededication in 1994. Since 2016, it has been styled Reynolds Army Health Clinic. (Courtesy of Reynolds Army Health Clinic Public Affairs Office.)

Seven

The Mission Enhanced

With the end of the Cold War, events overseas compelled America to remain involved in international affairs. The Middle East flamed as Saddam Hussein committed aggression against the tiny country of Kuwait. Operations Desert Shield and Desert Storm forced Hussein to retreat back into Iraq. Fort Sill made a sizable contribution in terms of men and firepower, furnishing the "steel rain" that put enemy soldiers to flight.

The years that followed were replete with intensive training and continued weapons development. Fort Sill participated in writing new doctrine for the post–Cold War world based upon power projection of military forces from the United States and massive amounts of field artillery firepower.

Military aviation was further developed, as aerial platforms were devised to target and engage the enemy. Complete weapons systems were developed and deployed to counter potential enemies in the shortest possible time, regardless of where conflict might arise.

Base Realignment and Closure (BRAC) in 2005 dramatically realigned military installations to save money, eliminate duplication of resources, and maximize and concentrate complementary assets. Over 100 military installations were closed, but Fort Sill survived and thrived when the Air Defense Artillery School moved from Fort Bliss, Texas, to join the Field Artillery School at Fort Sill and form the Fires Center of Excellence for fires training, including training Marine artillerymen.

In 2003, Fort Sill proved itself as a premier power projection installation by its participation in Operation Enduring Freedom in Afghanistan and Operation Iraqi Freedom by sending field artillery units to Southwest Asia to destroy the Taliban and free the Iraqis from the tyrannical yoke of Saddam Hussein. In 2011, the Fires Center of Excellence became a reality through the guidance of the Joint Chiefs of Staff and Maj. Gen. David D. Halverson of Fort Sill.

With a dramatically increased allotment of personnel, military housing was accordingly increased. Several additional barracks, dining halls, and facilities of all kinds arose. These have included recreational, educational, medical and dental, and other facilities to meet the needs of the soldiers and their families.

In 2018, Fort Sill has come a long way since the days of the Old West. It has matured in modern wars. Its leaders and personnel have made the commitment and sacrifices necessary to safeguard not only American liberty and freedom but also that of the free world.

The M109 self-propelled howitzer served for many years as a highly mobile rapid-firing tube artillery system of 155-millimeter caliber. Together with its M992 armored ammunition carrier, the weapon system eliminated targets with conventional shells over 11 miles. In addition, rocket-assisted munitions were provided that ranged up to 19 miles. Both vehicles could attain speeds of 35 miles per hour. They appear in action during Desert Storm in 1991.

The M270 multiple launch rocket system (MLRS) was designed as an armored, highly mobile, self-propelled multi-rocket launcher. First adopted in 1983, over 1,300 were built in succeeding years. It has been fielded by numerous allied nations in addition to performing sterling service for the US military. This shot is from a firing practice around 1985. (Courtesy of US Army Artillery Museum.)

MLRS proved one of the hardest hitters of Operation Desert Storm. Its salvos of lethal clusters of munitions were aptly referred to as "steel rain" by friend and foe alike. The Army Tactical Missile System was an alternate system operating on the same principles but with a heavier, farther-ranging, and more precise guided weapon.

The spiritual needs of the Fort Sill community have resulted in several on-post chapels. The Grierson Hall Chapel was constructed on Grierson Hill, named for the first post commander. Protestant and Roman Catholic services have been conducted at this location. Indeed, military chaplains have increased in number, serving many faiths. This view is from around 1991. (Courtesy of US Army Artillery Museum.)

Key Gate has been the primary entry for longer than memory can serve, maybe since the c. 1918 trolley service to Lawton. In this scene, an M101 105-millimeter howitzer helps to welcome returning soldiers as well as their dependents and many visitors. The time is about 1992, when Fort Sill won several consecutive annual awards for excellence. (Courtesy of US Army Artillery Museum.)

A bronze 12-pounder cannon adds period flavor to the approaches of the Fort Sill Officers' Club, photographed in 1993. For many years, the club hosted numerous special events and was a cozy place to unwind with friends. It has been redesignated the Patriot Club, is accessible by enlisted personnel as well as officers, and of this printing, is a welcome resort for Army retirees, dependents, and many members of the civilian workforce. (Courtesy of US Army Artillery Museum.)

Artillerymen of C Battery, 1st Battalion, 321st Airborne Field Artillery Regiment, fire on an enemy target on July 6, 2009, using an M777 155-millimeter howitzer in Konar Province, Afghanistan. Their firing position is part of Forward Operating Base Bostick. (Courtesy of Spc. Evan Marcy, *Fort Sill Tribune*.)

Air defenders of the 32nd Army Air and Missile Defense Command Patriot Battery launch their warbird during a combined live-fire exercise on July 11, 2011, at McGregor Range, New Mexico. All missiles successfully engaged their targets. (Courtesy of Rick Nielson, *Fort Sill Tribune*.)

At the Field Artillery Basic Officer Leader Course, 2nd Lts. Brett Olmsted (left) and Richard Peterson provide target information to a tactical operations center during their class capstone exercise on December 11, 2014. This was performed near Contingency Operations Location Mow-Way Range, Fort Sill. (Courtesy of Jeff Crawley, *Fort Sill Tribune*.)

Senior leaders of the 2nd Battalion, 2nd Field Artillery Regiment, take part in competitive physical training at Lake Elmer Thomas Recreation Area, Fort Sill, on April 29, 2015. The soldiers performed a one-mile simulated combat run, then raced their Zodiac boats to determine the fastest team. (Courtesy of Marie Berberea, *Fort Sill Tribune*.)

A Marine artillery crew fires an M777 howitzer during a training exercise on February 4, 2016, at Quanah Range, Fort Sill. Marines from as far away as California and Japan fired new precision guidance kit smart-fused 155-millimeter shells capable of dropping a round within 30 meters of its intended target. (Courtesy of Cindy McIntyre, *Fort Sill Tribune*.)

S.Sgts. Jorge Loera (center) and Jose Hernandez ram a 155-millimeter shell into the chamber of an M777 howitzer. S.Sgt. Alex Rodenhaber stands ready to insert the propellant increment sleeve. (Courtesy of Cindy McIntyre, *Fort Sill Tribune*.)

An Army National Guard basic combat trainee in the split option program from C Battery, 1st Battalion, 79th Field Artillery Regiment, successfully negotiates a rope. The training was performed at Treadwell Tower, Fort Sill, on May 30, 2017. (Courtesy of Cindy McIntyre, *Fort Sill Tribune*.)

PFC Rachel Dibbins leads 2nd Platoon, C Battery, 1st Battalion, 79th Field Artillery Regiment, in cadence as it marches to the dining facility during White Phase of basic combat training. Dibbins was selected as platoon guide on June 18, 2017. As such, she took on responsibility formerly reserved to drill sergeants. (Courtesy of Cindy McIntyre, *Fort Sill Tribune*.)

S.Sgt. Joseph Dupee, 5th Battalion, 5th Air Defense Regiment, reconnects with his daughters, six-year-old Caitlin and three-year-old Marissa, during a redeployment ceremony at Rinehart Fitness Center on July 19, 2017. Dupee's unit returned from Iraq and Afghanistan, where their missions included counter rocket, artillery, and mortar during their nine-month deployment. (Courtesy of Cindy McIntyre, *Fort Sill Tribune*.)

Eight

The Past Lives On

Fort Sill has an engaging history. Where else can be found such fascinating personalities as Geronimo, Harry Truman, Henry Flipper, Benjamin and Alice Grierson, and Morse and Ambrosia Taylor, and such landmarks as Medicine Bluffs, Geronimo's grave, the Sherman House, and the Balloon Hangar, to name but a few?

Lt. (later colonel) W.S. Nye wrote the history of Fort Sill—*Carbine and Lance* remains the standard history to this day. M.Sgt. Morris Swett wrote an invaluable history in 1921. In 1934, Lt. (later colonel) Harry C. Larter established the museum on post and served as its first curator. Other significant curators have been Gillett Griswold, Towana Spivey, Gordon Blaker, and Dr. Scott Neel.

In the 1990s, Maj. Gen. Leo J. Baxter shared a wider vision and greater role for the museum, which already served as a post museum as well as the branch museum for field artillery. Col. (later major general) Mark McDonald mapped the way and implemented the directorate concept, whereby three museums were coordinated by one supervisor, Frank Siltman.

The original post museum has an outstanding Native American collection, Western art, and frontier military weapons and artifacts, and includes a growing African American Buffalo Soldier emphasis. The artillery museum has an enviable collection highlighting all periods of American artillery. Last but not least, there is the intriguing Air Defense Artillery Learning Center, with its array of antiaircraft and antimissile weapons of all kinds. Relocated from Fort Bliss, Texas, the Air Defense Artillery Learning Center was developed by curator Jonathan Bernstein.

Around post, the historic sites are ubiquitous. The historic landmark district features over two dozen original structures interpreted by the museum visitor center with a theater, exhibits, brochures, and audio recordings. Outside the landmark district are nearby and far-flung buildings, parks, and a variety of commemorative sites.

Frequent living history events enliven a visit to Fort Sill. Old-time baseball games, including an authentic Fort Sill Indian team, historical reenactments, and the Candlelight Stroll near the holidays, always prove popular with the community and visitors at large.

At present, visitors must obtain a pass from the Fort Sill Visitor Center, but this is not difficult, with signage well posted for access to the post. A visit to Fort Sill is educational and enjoyable for all who wish to explore the past and contemplate the future.

The Fort Sill Museum pursued two major missions for almost 75 years: the preservation and interpretation of Fort Sill material culture and history, and the field artillery branch of service. One memorable feature of the mid-20th century was the Cannon Walk, supplemented by the Missile Park, seen here as it was developed about 1985. The guided missile shown is a Corporal. (Courtesy of US Army Artillery Museum.)

Maj. Gen. Mark McDonald contributed to the historic legacy of Fort Sill. In 2005, as chief of staff, then-Colonel McDonald implemented plans for reorganizing the museums on post as a directorate to maximize resources, including staffing. The plan was so sound that a few years later, as commanding general of Fort Sill, he finalized arrangements by adding the Air Defense Artillery Learning Center to the other two museums, that of Old Post and Field Artillery. He facilitated growth by the innovative use of new weapons parks as well as large, temporary buildings. (Courtesy of John D. Beemer, Fires Center of Excellence Protocol.)

Medicine Bluffs have always been both historically and spiritually significant. They are sacred to the American Indian tribes of the area. Four contiguous bluffs rise above Medicine Bluff Creek, a tributary of Cache Creek and the Red River. The highest bluff surmounts a sheer cliff 310 feet tall. A rock cairn built by medicine men was discovered atop its crest by soldiers who visited the site in 1869. (Courtesy of Peter Contos.)

Sherman House continues to serve as the living quarters of the commanding officer and first lady of Fort Sill. Built of native limestone, it is safeguarded as a national historic site, remembered as the scene of a dramatic confrontation between Gen. William T. Sherman and several Kiowa war chiefs in 1871. (Courtesy of Peter Contos.)

The Picket House is the oldest remaining structure at Fort Sill. It has been preserved to resemble its original appearance: a whitewashed frame building with the boards forming the walls situated upright like a picket fence. Today, it houses the administrative offices of the director of museums at Fort Sill. (Courtesy of Peter Contos.)

The middle cavalry barracks have been preserved and restored so that authentic replica furnishings enable the visitor to experience the atmosphere of the off-duty surroundings of frontier soldiers. The southernmost cavalry barracks still feature the doors leading into the basement (now stoned up), where prisoners were detained, including Kiowa war chiefs. (Courtesy of Peter Contos.)

The Stone Corral is such a formidable-looking structure that many have mistaken it for the principal strongpoint of early Fort Sill. It was erected to protect the mules and horses pulling the wagons that supplied the early garrison. At times it has featured special events and exhibits, including a Native American tepee. (Courtesy of Peter Contos.)

The original hospital was built in 1871, and although surrounded by wings and additional structures, it remains recognizable. Inside, some of the rooms retain the aura of soldier patients of long ago. (Courtesy of Peter Contos.)

The band quarters building, known as Wichita House, was refurbished at the suggestion of Fort Sill first lady Connie McDonald in 2010. Guests in these quarters experience the ambience of frontier military heritage with modern convenience. (Courtesy of Peter Contos.)

The Old Guardhouse for years was called the "Geronimo Hotel," though inaccurately. Although Geronimo was detained here on a few occasions, the stays were always brief and uneventful. The building held many kinds of prisoners through the years, but it had a more positive history after 1934: it was the beginning of the Fort Sill Museum. (Courtesy of Peter Contos.)

The post chapel was built in 1875 and remains little altered aside from a vestry on the north side. A beautiful stained-glass portrayal of Saint Barbara can be enjoyed during daylight hours. Religious services continue here, the second-oldest place of worship in the state of Oklahoma. (Courtesy of Peter Contos.)

Laundress quarters, affectionately styled Soapsuds Row, consist of small duplexes just west of the cavalry barracks. Laundresses were so prized by the lonely soldiers that many agreed to early marriages. This upset the commanding officer so much that he ordered subsequent laundresses to be recruited from the homeliest women the recruiting officer could find. (Courtesy of Peter Contos.)

Flipper's Ditch commemorates the drainage system Lt. Henry O. Flipper installed about 1878. The fevers associated with myriad gnats, flies, and mosquitoes subsided after this engineering feat. It has become a national historic site associated with the experiences of the Buffalo Soldiers of the Old West. (Courtesy of Peter Contos.)

Ambrosia Springs is off the beaten path but significant to many visitors. This limestone structure recalls the unselfish life of Ambrosia Taylor, wife of the post surgeon in the mid-1880s. Adjacent to Medicine Bluffs Creek, it is picturesque amidst dense woods. (Courtesy of Peter Contos.)

Geronimo's grave is visited by tens of thousands every year. A famed medicine man and freedom fighter, he was a symbol of resistance to the world of the white man. This Apache cemetery contains the final resting places of Geronimo's family members and many of his warriors. (Courtesy of Peter Contos.)

The first School of Fire for Field Artillery was a building previously assigned to mule packers. Commandant Dan T. Moore's office has been convincingly re-created; the classroom and office of the master sergeant have been restored as well. (Courtesy of Peter Contos.)

Chief's Knoll, called by some the "Indian Arlington," is a portion of the original Fort Sill Cemetery containing the graves of 15 famed chiefs and leaders of the Kiowa, Comanche, Kiowa-Apache, and Arapaho tribes. Established in 1869, it is also the burial place of post interpreter Horace P. Jones and the first soldier who died here, Pvt. Jesse Bicheres, who succumbed to illness soon after the post was founded. (Courtesy of Peter Contos.)

This glass-topped wall is near the northwest corner of the OPQ. By 1935, the nurses' quarters were completed and occupied. Off-duty soldiers regularly sat on this wall, whistling and calling endearments to the nurses. A new commander acted to end the merriment. He directed the sergeant major to organize a work detail: broken beer bottles were gathered from the post dump, and the sharp shards of glass were embedded all along the wall. No one has been seen sitting here since. (Courtesy of Peter Contos.)

The Balloon Hangar is the premier aviation historic site at Fort Sill. From 1935 to 1943, observation balloons were operated from this hangar. It was determined that, because of sudden, unexpected winds, if a prototype could operate successfully here, the production model would be able to cope with adverse winds anywhere. (Courtesy of Peter Contos.)

The Artillery Bowl is an open-air amphitheater constructed by the Works Progress Administration. American servicemen and -women have been entertained at this site by such luminaries as Louis Armstrong, Bob Hope, and many others. Spectator sports such as boxing have also been popular. (Courtesy of Peter Contos.)

On October 14, 2016, history came to life as Fort Sill Museum staff and volunteers presented Frontier Army Days. A Buffalo Soldier and 10th Cavalryman, Cpl. Ken Reese, described the weapons and equipment, plus the rigors of life both on campaign and in garrison to visitors young and old. Other interpreters shared their stories as they portrayed other soldiers, laundresses, schoolteachers, doctors, and even children on the Western frontier. (Courtesy of Cindy McIntyre, *Fort Sill Tribune*.)

The Gentle Tamers are the ladies, together with their children, associated with the living history program of the Fort Sill Museum. Pictured from left to right are Michele Mabry, Nathan Warnock, Katherine Grogan, Kim Warnock, Katie Warnock, and Alma Shappell. They portray members of Soapsuds Row, responsible for doing the laundry of the soldiers assigned to the fort. (Courtesy of Cindy McIntyre, *Fort Sill Tribune*.)

A preeminent Buffalo Soldier, Sgt. Wallace Moore is a recognized living historian of southwest Oklahoma. Utilizing stories and original poetry, he has educated audiences of all ages in subjects ranging from frontier military history and cowboys to 19th-century Seminole freedmen and more. Frequently, he has used the restored cavalry barracks for a historic setting. (Courtesy of Cindy McIntyre, *Fort Sill Tribune*.)

On December 10, 2016, the annual Candlelight Stroll provided visitors with a glimpse of the interior of the original buildings of the OPQ and numerous characters one might happen to meet. Robert McClain is a veteran museum volunteer who provides a compelling impression of a 10th Cavalry Buffalo Soldier. He wears the M1872 sergeant of cavalry sack coat and the post–Civil War forage cap, complete with crossed sabers. (Courtesy of Cindy McIntyre, *Fort Sill Tribune.*)

Participants include guides like Correy Twilley (left), wearing the M1872 undress uniform for a lieutenant of the 11th Infantry Regiment. His companion, Zane Mohler, wears the high-collared, form-fitting shell jacket of a cavalry private. Their tour group consists of about 20 visitors escorted by these stalwarts armed with candlelit lanterns. (Courtesy of Cindy McIntyre, *Fort Sill Tribune.*)

This hostess of Sherman House is Lori Siltman, who portrays Fort Sill's original first lady, Alice Grierson. She wears the elegant dress with hooped skirt fashionable in the 1870s. The house interior reflects the furniture, furnishings, and unique heritage of the quarters of the post commander and his wife from those earliest days to the present. (Courtesy of Cindy McIntyre, *Fort Sill Tribune*.)

The Old Post Chapel also recalls fond memories. Rev. Frank Hall Wright, a missionary to the Indians around Fort Sill, is portrayed by someone looking suspiciously like the author. The scene is the interior of the original chapel, complete with a Christmas tree sporting period-style decorations. (Courtesy of Cindy McIntyre, *Fort Sill Tribune*.)

The US Army Artillery Museum has an amazing assortment of artillery and missiles, as seen in this view of the self-propelled Pershing II missile, an effective deterrent to aggression during the Cold War. The weapons park is one of the most extensive of its kind in the world, but don't miss the exhibits and programs offered inside the museum. (Courtesy of Peter Contos.)

The Air Defense Artillery Learning Center also has an impressive array of American and foreign weapons both in its outdoors weapons park and inside the exhibit facilities. Here on display are Nike Ajax and Nike Hercules, weapons from the Cold War designed to intercept long-range enemy missiles and destroy them before they reached their targets. (Courtesy of Peter Contos.)

The Fort Sill Half Section is a highly mobile ceremonial and honors unit that features active-duty artillerymen wearing vintage uniforms as they maneuver and fire salutes with a World War I–era French 75 field gun. Expertly managed warhorses complete the drama and pageantry of their demonstrations. (Courtesy of John D. Beemer, Fires Center of Excellence Office of Protocol.)

The Fort Sill Museum is open to the public from 9:00 a.m. to 5:00 p.m. Tuesday through Saturday. Admission is free to the public. Passes are required for persons over 16 years of age, with a brief screening by the Fort Sill Visitor Center. The museums are closed on the Thanksgiving, Christmas, and New Year's holidays. For information on tours, research assistance, or donations, contact:

Fort Sill Museum Visitor Center
435 Quanah Road
Fort Sill, OK 73503-5100
580-442-5123